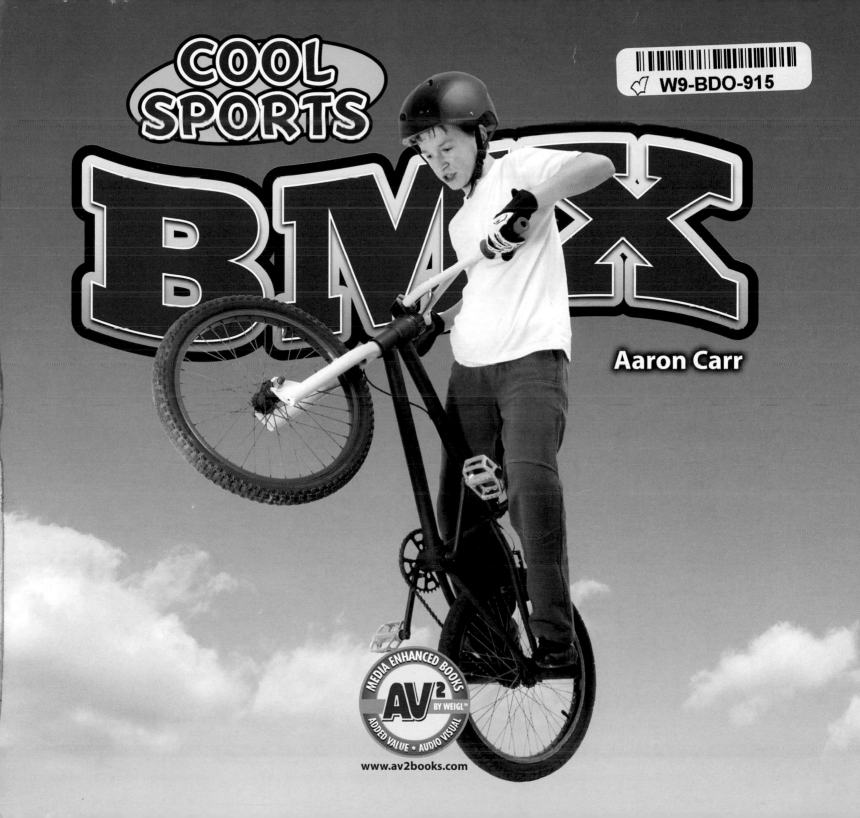

COOL SPORTS

BMX

Aaron Carr

LET'S READ
AV²
BY WEIGL™
ADDED VALUE • AUDIO VISUAL

Go to **www.av2books.com**, and enter this book's unique code.

BOOK CODE

R 8 6 3 4 3 0

AV² by Weigl brings you media enhanced books that support active learning.

AV² provides enriched content that supplements and complements this book. Weigl's AV² books strive to create inspired learning and engage young minds in a total learning experience.

Your AV² Media Enhanced books come alive with...

Audio
Listen to sections of the book read aloud.

Video
Watch informative video clips.

Embedded Weblinks
Gain additional information for research.

Try This!
Complete activities and hands-on experiments.

Key Words
Study vocabulary, and complete a matching word activity.

Quizzes
Test your knowledge.

Slide Show
View images and captions, and prepare a presentation.

... and much, much more!

Published by AV² by Weigl
350 5th Avenue, 59th Floor, New York, NY 10118
Website: www.av2books.com   www.weigl.com

Library of Congress Cataloguing in Publication data available upon request.
Fax 1-866-449-3445 for the attention of the Publishing Records department.

ISBN 978-1-61913-510-9 (hard cover)
ISBN 978-1-61913-516-1 (soft cover)

Printed in the United States of America in North Mankato, Minnesota
1 2 3 4 5 6 7 8 9   16 15 14 13 12

042012
WEP050412

Editor: Aaron Carr   Art Director: Terry Paulhus

Weigl acknowledges Getty Images as the primary image supplier for this title.

COOL SPORTS

BMX

CONTENTS

BMX means bicycle moto X. People use BMX bikes for racing, jumping, and doing tricks.

BMX bikes are small and light. Some BMX bikes are made to do jumps and tricks. Others are made for racing.

Pro BMX riders do tricks with their bikes.

BMX riders should always wear a helmet. Helmets keep riders safe when they fall.

Pro BMX riders wear helmets, knee pads, and gloves.

People can ride BMX bikes in many places. Some people ride on dirt trails. Others ride in skateparks.

Like a PRO

Pro BMX riders use different kinds of tracks and parks.

BMX riders have to practice often. This helps them become good at BMX riding.

Like a PRO

Pro BMX riders practice for many hours each day.

BMX riders go down a large ramp and jump over a big gap.
This is called Big Air.

Like a PRO

Pro Big Air riders get points for the best trick.

BMX riders do many tricks in a U-shaped ramp. This is called Vert.

Pro Vert riders try to land many big tricks.

BMX riders go through a skatepark doing jumps and tricks. This is called Park.

Like a PRO

Pro Park riders try to come up with new tricks.

19

The best BMX riders from all around the world compete in the X Games.

Many people come to watch the BMX riders do big jumps and tricks.

BMX FACTS

These pages provide detailed information that expands on the interesting facts found in this book. These pages are intended to be used by adults as a learning support to help young readers round out their knowledge of each sport in the *Cool Sports* series.

Pages 4–5

BMX means bicycle moto X. People use BMX bikes for racing, jumping, and doing tricks.

BMX is a sport that requires skill, determination, and focus. Athletes ride on specially designed bicycles on various types of terrain. There are many styles of BMX riding. In BMX racing, riders race on dirt tracks with many jumps and turns. In freestyle, riders perform tricks. Other types of BMX include Street, Park, Vert, Dirt, Big Air, and Flatland.

Pages 6–7

BMX bikes are small and light. Some BMX bikes are made to do jumps and tricks. Others are made for racing.

Pro BMX riders do tricks with their bikes.

BMX bikes are designed to be lightweight and strong. This helps people perform big jumps and tricks without damaging the bike. BMX bikes usually have large wheels, about 18 to 24 inches (46 to 61 centimeters) wide. Racing bikes are often made of lightweight aluminum. Freestyle bikes need to be stronger to withstand the force of landing jumps and tricks. They weigh about twice as much as racing bikes.

Pages 8–9

BMX riders should always wear a helmet. Helmets keep riders safe when they fall.

Pro BMX riders wear helmets, knee pads, and gloves.

The helmet is the most important piece of safety equipment. When falling off a bike, the rider's head could hit the ground. Helmets have saved many riders from serious head injuries. Most riders also wear knee pads and elbow pads. Riders can break their wrists if they try to break a fall with their hands. Instead, riders learn how to use their knee pads and elbow pads to cushion a fall.

Pages 10–11

People can ride BMX bikes in many places. Some people ride on dirt trails. Others ride in skateparks.

Pro BMX riders use different kinds of tracks and parks.

People can ride BMX bikes almost anywhere. Skateparks, dirt trails, and vacant lots are great places for riders to practice their moves. Many freestyle BMX riders practice at skateparks. Here, there are obstacles that they can use to perform tricks. Flatland riders remain in one place as they balance, twist, and spin on their bikes. Racers speed around dirt tracks.

Pages 12–13

Practice is the most important part of becoming good at any sport. Most professional BMX riders practice for many hours every day. They have to practice the same moves many times to make sure they can perform well in competitions. BMX riders also experiment with new tricks and riding styles to improve their skills.

Pages 14–15

In Big Air, riders go off a megaramp, which features an 80-foot (24-meter) drop. Riders go down the drop and launch off a quarterpipe and into the air. They then fly through the air over a 70-foot (21-m) gap. Riders perform an aerial trick before landing on the other side of the gap. They continue down another ramp and over another quarterpipe before doing a final trick.

Pages 16–17

During the Vert, or vertical, event, BMX riders perform a series of tricks while riding back and forth in a halfpipe. The halfpipe is usually 153-feet (47-m) wide and 11-feet (3-m) high. Each rider gets two 60-second runs to impress the judges. Riders score points for style and the difficulty and creativity of their tricks. The rider with the most points wins.

Pages 18–19

Park competitions take place on a course similar to a skatepark. The course has many obstacles that riders can use. Riders each get 75 seconds to go through the course and impress the judges with their skills. Riders can use an obstacle in any way they want. Obstacles include ramps, quarterpipes, and rails. Riders earn points for style, originality, and the difficulty of their tricks.

Pages 20–21

The Summer X Games is an annual sports tournament that showcases the best athletes in the extreme sports world. The X Games started in 1995. The competition includes events for BMX, skateboarding, moto X, and rallycross. The X Games attract the best extreme athletes from around the world each year. Some events feature athletes flying 40 feet (12 m) above the ground.

KEY WORDS

Research has shown that as much as 65 percent of all written material published in English is made up of 300 words. These 300 words cannot be taught using pictures or learned by sounding them out. They must be recognized by sight. This book contains 60 common sight words to help young readers improve their reading fluency and comprehension. This book also teaches young readers several important content words. These words are paired with pictures to aid in learning and improve understanding.

Page	Sight Words First Appearance	Page	Content Words First Appearance
4	and, for, means, people, use	4	bicycle, bikes, BMX, jumping, moto x, racing, tricks
6	are, do, light, made, others, small, some, to	6	jumps
7	a, like, their, with	7	riders
8	always, keep, should, they, when	8	helmet
10	can, in, many, on, places	9	gloves, knee pads
11	different, kinds, of	10	skateparks, trails
12	at, good, have, helps, often, them	11	parks, tracks
13	day, each	13	hours
14	big, down, go, is, large, over, this	14	Big Air, gap, ramp
15	get, points, the	16	Vert
17	land, try	18	Park
18	here, through	20	X Games
19	come, new, up		
20	all, around, from, watch, world		

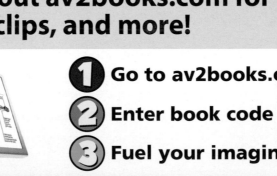